Simona is a Romanian-born pu ... living in UK, where she enjoys her profession as a radiographer and writing, as her biggest passion. Being a woman, a daughter, a sister, a mother, an expat, a Transylvanian, and a Londoner now, she is taking the sight to the personal life experience with a social writing touch.

For Dave.

Simona Prilogan

CARVING MAGIC

AUSTIN MACAULEY PUBLISHERS™

LONDON • CAMBRIDGE • NEW YORK • SHARJAH

A CIP catalogue record for this title is available from the British Library.

ISBN 9781398491199 (Paperback)
ISBN 9781398491205 (ePub e-book)

www.austinmacauley.com

First Published 2023
Austin Macauley Publishers Ltd®
1 Canada Square
Canary Wharf
London
E14 5AA

Heartiest thanks to my family for creating the most significant impetus for my poetry journey. My sons, Cristian and Cosmin have been the most significant advocates and supporters of my writing.

Deepest thanks to my special friend Abid, for his help with editing, as well as for great support and encouragement.

Warmest thanks to the amazing and talented artist Cristina Stan, for drawing the wonderful illustrations for the book.

Many thanks to the editing and publishing team at Austin Macauley Publishers, for believing in my poetry, and for their priceless contribution.

Table of Contents

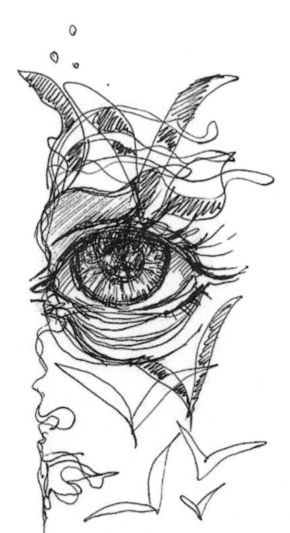

Eve

I'm colouring love with joy from above,
With smiles from my dawns enriching life's lawns,
In light's sweet embrace, surrounded by grace.
From minty pipe dreams, I set aiming streams.
From winters I bring the quietness' string.
Regaining the strength from bright snowy land.
I'm spring to my earth, nurturing rebirth.
Still childlike sometimes, I'm puzzles of rhymes.
Revealing the art, my eyes speak my heart.
Fragile like a rose, yet strong in purpose,
I'm colouring love with bless from above.

I Came From

I came from a colourful town,
Set down amongst the hills of charming Transylvania,
Awakening by the steel plant's sirens singing their calls,
At each 6 then 7 o'clock in the mornings.
The dense smog, and metallic dust, were twirling their
shadowing blues,
Till the windows of our 10th floor apartment

I came from a communist plan,
Creating some sort of brilliant future,
Where children would not be of their parents,
But belong to the country,
Listening to commands of totalitarianism.

I came from a state of nonsense
Creating bewilderment in the brains,
Throwing Gods in the bin of history,
Arguing that the old time is junk in itself,
Yet grandparents seeking to save jewels of land's culture.

I came from a red zone flaming the worker parents,
With sentences that discourage the success,
Quarrelling the idea of not being the same, but inferior.

I came from the classrooms where some teachers will try their best,
Not to bring out the communist party's cruelty,
But drawing our attention to the beautiful patterns of Fibonacci,
And the harmony of classical arts.

I came from the 23rd of August parades,
The hilarious circus of reality,
Learning how disguising would be our future vibe.

I came from the togetherness,
Smashing the walls of communism,
But stolen by the contemporary bloodshed.

I'm Holding

I'm holding,
These memories painfully crushing my dawns,
When freedom was captured in terror's homelands.
For finding the pace, the truth, the solace,
I'm fully aware I might need to dare,
Admitting my pain, again and again,
Waltzing together in this stormy weather,
So, we can both tie, releasing the cry.
Accepting the past, the smog, and the dust
I'm strong as a feather,
Yet able to bend for reaching the end
Of what fears penned.

I'm holding.
The lands of my thoughts, connecting the dots,
Between shadows' tones, while running alone,
Away from the dark, still carrying the mark,
Of murdering threat... forgive, not forget.
Yet learning to spell the peace in its shell.

I Carry with Me

I carry with me my parents' art chart,
From their strongest stories penned deep in heart.
With prayers at dawns for keeping me well,
With kindness and joy gleaming the shell.

I carry with me my mom's calming pace,
For rounding to peace my only solace,
When skies pull away their blue, and their stars,
Are dripping the doubts all over my scars.

I carry with me my father's firm bones,
Carved in my flesh, ridding the stones,
Of burdens and wrongs at life's darker gates,
Smoothing the paths dropping the weights.

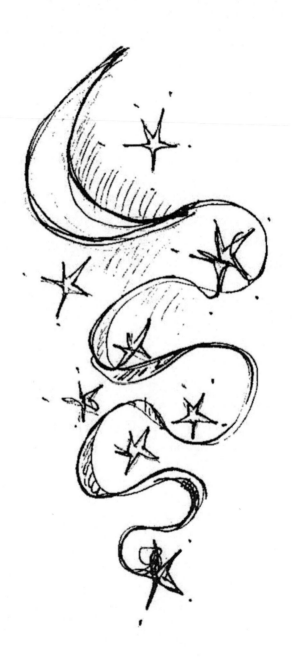

Dreams Onset

Behind the smiling flowers, behind the golden stars,
I sensed in peculiar paths the bridge up to my peace.
I'm still behind the shadows, writing in other books,
A long poem to life whilst twirling with my tears.

When running in the dark of winter's nights to reach,
The warm embrace of mornings, abandoning the screams,
Of all the painful hours, still looking to my bridge,
I dare myself, while crafting the wings to deepest dreams.

As heavy rain is falling in all my winter days,
Dealing with a faker who just breaks out my faith,
I dare myself to wander through hopes and morning rays,
Ahead of lately hours, to catch the dream onset.

Waiting for the Cheerful Summer

Waiting for the cheerful summer,
I knelt at the rim of sorrow,
With a mystic scent of wonder,
Hugging tight plans for tomorrow,
Praying, hoping, thinking, sensing,
Magic scents out of desire.
Colours, fierce like blood, are setting,
Through my chest, the sacred fire.

I shall care for love you gave me,
'Till no summers will be dancing,
Memories blinking tears' quay
From a sea of the fate's glancing.
I shall dare the pain of sunsets,
Twisting sadness to fresh dawns,
Ruling out the rustling regrets,
Shrouded in biases' lawns.

I shall hold your thorny branches,
Wildly piercing my soft palms,
Witnessing how rosy patches,
Are renaming my new balm.
I shall keep the fire burning,

Deeply carving in my heart,
'Till the summers will be washing,
All the fears, somewhere apart.

In meantime I shall keep writing
Mathematics of the love,
Where foresight is greatly catching
Calculations from above.
Where the one adding another,
Is totalling still as one.
While the two minus the other,
Is equalling just a none.

Angels-Stars

The magic binds again the night,
As our hearts are carving love,
With mystic vibes rising above,
Enchanting stories, rich and bright.
They take me always to the trails,
Revealing thoughts from saga's maze.
Shaping emotions on the ways,
The skies are pouring fairy tales.

This night the fireflies are hot,
Telling their story once again,
Crossing the deepest longing lane,
In name of love for what they sought.
The legend says that long ago,
When skies were shaping their extent,
The angels brought the magic scent,
Of sacred words for a fresh glow.

Beneath the blue, the earth set time,
Crafting emotions from God's spheres
Enriching beauty in green squares
Through sparking beams of the life's rhyme.
A choir of angels paid their psalms,

Across the seas, mountains, grasslands
In contemplating humankind,
Among their colourful, broad farms.

They fell in love with what they found,
Nuances, flavours, songs, perfumes,
The vibes, the touches, insights, tunes
Of a togetherness earthbound.
One of the angels saw the eyes,
Of a delightful shepherd girl,
Learning how love might be the pearl,
Brought by the gods from seven skies.

The angels' chorus penned few lines,
As only love could rhyme and sing,
While God was sensing their lust's spring
Nostalgic burning in their eyes.
Their songs were powerful, and tend,
To spread their sympathy around.
Matching the space, the love was found,
To have the rich strength to ascend.

The fate was turning a rebirth:
To ease their longing tenderness,
Divinity gave them the chance,
To always look to the green earth.
The story said how in one night,
Those angels were reborn as stars,
Caring their beams from the sky's bars,
Nurturing faithfully the light.
The angel-star who fell too deep,

For the enchanting shepherd's eyes,
Was still expressive over skies,
Yearning her look beyond the weep.
After a while, sensing his cries,
God sent him straight, in speed, to ground,
Twisting the destiny around,
Into a thousand fireflies.

The saga's penning till today,
How fireflies are bright in night,
Lighting for shepherd girl the sight,
So, she could see his loving way.
The skies are covering the night,
With thousands of angel-stars above,
Who stay trustworthy in their love,
For beauty of the humankind.

In Art's Freedom Square

Drawing lines between the thoughts,
Puzzled in a freedom's square,
Where the colours become worlds,
For the stories to be shared.
There is not a silent shade,
But a passion and a dare.

Crafting dreams from what seems gone,
Broken in a misty tale,
Twisting sorrow to fresh dawn,
With the hues from the faith's trail,
Where the memories enfold,
Zesty sagas to be told.

Painting joy beneath the skies
Where the peace is having tea,
Dressed in love, so bright and wise,
Days are finding the new me.
Shaping art among my hands,
Deeply carving freedom's lands.

Carving Magic

Mornings beat with faster speed,
Which are sparking the designs,
Through wide space, big points, and signs,
All together minding lines,
Things to measure right the need.

Days empowering the light,
To acknowledge truth that stands,
For the world to take on hands,
Sense for shaping dreamy lands.
Gleam may spark in every sight.

Counting rational ahead,
Steps, ideas, yet rephrase,
The entire mind through space,
I may dare the knowledge base,
And uplift my vision head.

Drawing loops over the moon,
Flaming thoughts outside the box,
Shaping wisdom in deep talks,
Carving magic in my rocks,
Bluntly voicing insight's tune.

Windows

The castle constantly was deeming my morning glance
From the hat of the hill as I smiled to it.
Apple trees were embracing the place with their branches
Like a warm hug in a vintage capsule.
The wind smoothly brought the flowers blooming perfume
While my thoughts waltzed with the old warrior's mind
Who has gone beyond the blue limits
Leaving behind all the glorious stories
Enclosed between the stones, gardens, and tunnels.

The scents of old days reached my windows
Speaking their struggle out
In a serene symphony of remembrance,
While next to the fort,
The steel plant made up the reality
Through the intense smoke, dust, and wonder.

The past was still picturing the ideas in the present's core
Yet another war at my windows
Was murdering my vision in the evening's dusk.
The nights covered the horizon
With a murky pillow.
No stars to come yet

To rescue hope from the blackness
In all those frozen hours.
Childhood was silently passing the caves,
Gazing to freedom windows
Set off in the future's square.
Dreams swung the yearning at the castle door
Playing cards with karma
Over the communism's eyes.

Nowadays the steel plant is only a reminiscence
At my windows glance.
An empty city regards the mornings.
A modern war
Is still blurring children's vision.
Everything is new but seemingly passing the bridge
Between then and now.

Today's core is a mirror reflecting the past
Through another smoke, dust, and wander.
The same desire is flying through time,
To love and be loved 'till reaching happiness.
Anything else are just the colours' stories.

In all this contemporary bloodshed
Peace remains the Cinderella
Looking through the inner windows.

It's Getting Too Windy

Habibi, it's getting too windy outside
And rain waltzes again with the flames of memory.
Between my thoughts, your smile
Brings force from a blurry past
Depicting the hope within those dreams
Where harmony was the valley's queen
Running barefoot in the grass of happiness,
Playing its flute in our hugs
'Till sunsets were wrapping the tenderness in lust
Worrying nothing for tomorrow's glance.

Live out the moment and keep strong!
You used to murmur in my ears
So we may not fear the bombing attack
Madly striking at the front door of our entire future.
Let's sing today, my dear, I always said,
For the chirping birds to join us,
Bringing the blissful heaven upon us.

It's getting too windy outside, my beloved
Whispers unravelled in the past
Still I know that your smile is very much alive
Between the sunset's drops of rain

Washing my fears away,
For the love to be wrapped around my heart
'Till angels bring peace from the skies.

Sad Songs

My childhood routine grew sad, grey, and blind
Through communism's space, vanquished sometimes
With songs of the fears, with hope knelt behind
The tears in the dark, torturing the mind.
The freedom was something we haven't yet seen
Just spotting what mind was eager to mean.

The faith overseen the eyes of terror
'Till God had been thrown in writ of error.
'Till angels were murdered between lies, and dark
Was lying its shelter in poverty's stark.

Today I may find the roots of peace
But fears override emotions through tears.
The sky is shifting my panic to calm,
Through deepest thoughts holding my head, in a balm
Of magical moments I may spark on eyes
But songs are still sad while falling apart.

Modern Deluge

This modern deluge kneeing my dreams
Twisting their blue, torturing my skies
Tearing their chant and pouring grief streams
Trying again to bleed yearning's eyes.
They call it free world while smashing behind
The light to adapt to their shadows' kind.

It Was Freezing on Those December Days

It was freezing on those December days
Painting my childhood routine
Between queues in food market
And classes in a cold room.
Yet the smiles of the teacher melted somehow, the anxiety;
A fear of not being good enough
For what communist party would establish
On behalf of my name.
What name? I surprised myself asking
Yet, *Shhhh, be quiet!* they said, *and keep going*
In this pecuniary rock and roll of the time.
Stones breaking hearts at the borders of humanity
Weren't new on the earth.

It was freezing on those December days
When a song of freedom touched the skies.
A choir of children singing it in the opera's square
Praying their thoughts, kneeling on the cathedral stairs.
Terrorist's alarm played instead the death game
Reddening the faith, bathing innocence in blood.
Angels were hovering above, shedding their eyes over us.

It was freezing on those December days
While I tried to negate
The name of murdering;
At the corner of imagination, another choir was singing
'Till brought the angels in the square
To teach us how freedom is spelt
In the souls' spring.

At the Borders of Humanity

I hid under the ground at the borders of mercy and unknown
The emptiness silently cried out its rage.
The days dropped down their fears
For the ones who were unalike shaped in beliefs.
The prejudices dressed their black robes
Paving with blood the whole nights streets.
Chanting the hate songs, its soldiers brought their hell on
earth.

I hid my childhood under the ground
At the borders of kindness
Where dolls played chess and bridges,
Reading for me the others' stories
Left behind of an evolved planet, lost for now
Under the bloodshed of genocide.
The hell's soldiers, *aiming to a right world*, squeezed the light
to adapt
To their hatred refrains 'till covered the righteous with death's
wings.

The angels were murdered in the town's squares
For brightening the arms of love
Yet their prayers touched the skies

''till the archangel's army taught us
How life is spelt in the humankind language.

I hid my memories in a hide-and-seek game
Where dolls are still alive through my space
Colouring the hope for the sake of humanity
Where I religiously accept each of our shapes
Hiding the fears, seeking the peace at the core of love.

I Wanna Go Home

To Sylvia, who is looking for her way back home while living in a care home.

I wanna go home
Is her name, her song, her tale
While mind is wandering through
All her missing space.
Memories spark on dusks
As time's eyes are tearing the minutes away.

I wanna go home,
The angels are healing the wounds
And birds are singing between
The spaces. *Now* and *then,* tightly dance
With childhood's fire 'till become as one
The last soldier of the flame.

I wanna go home,
The answer she whispers to walls
While watching the memories box
Looking for her lost story inside.
Abandoned in silence, she steps
Backwards in peculiar sand.

I wanna go home,
Painting hues of hope
Twirling the faith, falling
Behind the nights, behind the doors.
Another sweet dream may come to swing
The sadness. Or finding the way home.

She Packed in the Boxes,
the Hope

She packed in the boxes the hope
While tears were embracing her soul;
A new dawn was struggling to cope
What fear left for mornings. A whole
Of sadness behind of her stole.

She packed all her hurt remembrance
With valleys destroying the light
With shadows denying essence
Of truth wandering in the night
While honour subsided from the right.

Not only her mind, yet still more
The borders distorted the trust
In eyes of despair and the sore.
Today all the packs take the just
Of sheltering her from the dust.

She packed all the wishes as doves
Are bringing the peace through the skies,
While rain drives the love from above
Scenting the world from her eyes
A war from inside fades and dies.

Pray

I smile with force to catch the sun
Between the thoughts, to ray my path.
The sea yet tells me that the run
Is stuck in the misgivings bath.

Where angels pray to ease the pain
Of all the troubles in the world.
Where blue is looking for the rain
To wash the qualm from people's fort.

I quietly remain to pray
To find the peace in our way.

Christmas Lights

The Christmas lights are shining bright
Besides the buildings, thoughts, and dreams,
Through Oxford Street the shady nights
Are craving hopes on fancy's beams.
The money smell might crock the hearts
Too loud, too blind, too quick to fall
For something undefined in charts
Of a new normal drove in brawl.
Yet fairy lights are here indeed
To spark sweet memories and shine
For other stars to catch the deed
Beneath the skies, on Christmastime.

I keep my walk as a routine
Spicing the path with golden gleams,
Feeling the wind, an evergreen
Refreshing thoughts through winter's dreams.
The Regent Street keeps the old trick
In glossy stories, seraphs' spheres
The people's selfies click and flick
The smiles pretending happy cheers.
At Piccadilly Circus plays
A reality, converting dreams

Sleighing desire in a maze
One giving love while love receives.

The Christmas tree is wearing doubts
For the new vibes spacing the lines,
At Tottenham Court Road it sprouts
A homeless' camp pleading the slides.
At Primark's windows karma's game
Is chanting beggars' fooling songs,
Denying lives in dearth and shame,
Too stuck themselves in habits' wrong.
The antithesis strikes the eyes
Craving new thoughts for Santa's list
Through all the Holborn's stylish highs
My walk is carrying puzzle's mist.

The Christmas carols bring the tune
Of humankind wrapped up in love
From past is rising a nurture
Of a togetherness, above.
Yet Santa's sensing out of streets
Too full of people walking fast
The loneliness torturing beats
Of happiness losing its blast.
I wish I could drive Santa's sleigh
Through the pure lands of harmony,
Bringing compassion in the way,
A priceless gift at Christmas' tree.

The Poems I Wrote Yesterday

The poems I wrote yesterday
Became tears of longing, apart.
Today the sunset brought them back
In thousands of waves, looking for
My passion, my love, burnt away
In seven desires; a charm
Is chasing the breeze under the skies.

The poems I wrote yesterday
Became leaves, waltzing their fall.
Their spells spark the skyline and call
Those seven desires in mind
Till passion is getting its storm
With fevers and doubts running through
The whole universe, looking for
The magical lust of their rhymes.

The poems I wrote yesterday
Are wandering under the storms
Like *Ciara* is running through skies
Still looking for something may lost.
In seven desires, a fight
Is playing my heart and my soul

Like *Dennis* is tearing apart
The wounds over fears, 'till the ground
Is caressed by their tears from the fiery poems.

Tenderness

It's raining blue, my beloved!
Our windows laugh to the sky
Whilst the moon mysteriously binds
Its sapphires of longing and temptation.
It's raining wonder in ether.

The roses smile in the vase
Red floods our thoughts
And gives meaning
To this blue night's tenderness
Under this glorious sky.

It's raining wishes, it's raining green,
When time chooses to write down
The magic formulas from myths
That pour sour and burn away
All the sadness of sunsets.

It's raining colour, my beloved
It's raining songs, it's raining verse
Under this immense sky.

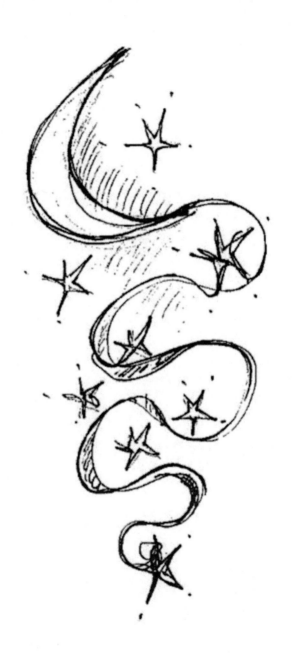

Joy

I think, you muse,
I want, you choose,
I feel, you pray,
I smile, you ray,
I laugh, you dare,
I game, you share
A shape in heart,
A form of art,
With happiness,
As a princess,
Sparking from skies,
Straight in my eyes.

I feel, you smile,
I dare, you file,
The marvel's gem,
As diadem,
For love to sing,
In our spring.

Charm

It's snowing the tales over us
With chapters surrounded by charm.
The evening is seizing the palm
Of seven desires. A spell
It's crossing in seconds, the path,
Just seven were those, yet apart
Some stings lost their battle duel.

It's raining the colours in verse
In seven nuances through rhymes,
Their songs bring the night in the cymes
With seven desirous bouquets
Of ardours from seven planets
Till blue turns on magical breeze
Like those seven shadings of seas.

While seven sunsets read to us
A story depicted from skies
Your warmth pens on stones seven highs
Of beauty of life, sensing care
Through seven sunrises we share
On our but unique love star
A fresh charm it's playing guitar.

Waltz of Lust

One, two, three…one, two, three…
Shall we feel, my beloved, the waltz of lust?

Three steps for the beauty of life,
Three steps through the grace on the way,
Fervour is bringing to us,
The vault of heaven…three steps…
Emotions are waltzing, my beloved,
Under this glorious azure,
Pouring delight through violin's spell.

A wind is dancing with us
Balancing the sounds between words,
Three steps for the allurement of soul,
Three steps through the melody of glow.
Under this majestic blue,
The strings are playing, my beloved,
Tying tenderness to magic.

Pitches and notes are embracing the floor
In a trip of sparking pirouettes,
A red is flooding the zest
Flaming ardour in our eyes.

Hope-Butterfly

Desire for trust
As run is a must
And days roll on grey
Ideas to sky.
When soul is expecting
The yearning to fly
I'm catching the eye
Of a hope-butterfly.

I'm painting my hall
While gleaming the soul.
Just wisdom and peace
Great love, to increase
And never to cry.

Raining Love

It's raining music from the skies
From blue it's pouring warm rejoice.
The tenderness is sprinkling voice
Of wander colouring the eyes.

It's raining love behind the fall
When rhapsody you play for me
Azure is lighting hearts to see
How fairy tales may spark their call.

Pouring the Rain

Pouring the rain over the lane
Walking the same path to the train
Of my deep thoughts which all may drive
Blue of the days into the rise.
Keeping the game, staying alive.
Smiling with force, letting behind.

Falling the drop over the hope
Washing instead what fears did
Over the skies, catching in flies
Doubts wings to rid, yet may forbid
Blinding past eyes, shaping the cries.
Yearning my hope, breaking the rope.

My thoughts in dance sparking their glance
Pouring the rain, washing my lane.

Colouring Dreams

A poem is falling away from the skies
Dressed in the drops sparking light
Straight in the rooms of my heart,
Feeding the hope through the cells
For tomorrows to catch up on dance
The beauty of all those sunsets
I've been dreaming about for a while.

Whisper to me kindly regards,
Dear wind, for the peace to get back
Singing through rhymes of this rain
Pairing the chances of pain
To get eased by love on its track.

Colouring dreams I might sleep
Under this rain pouring deep.

Flowering

They smile to left and beam to right
While straight ahead the joy rays light
Debating reality on plate
I might stay here twisting a fate
To catch the happiness perfume
Which flowers add to the day's resume
Forgetting worries from the streets
With fear's patterns between their tweets.
They smile to left and beam to right
Till grace is smoothing my insight.

Raining

It's raining again cats and dogs
Yet longing is flooding my vein
And flaming intensely my thoughts
Along with the rhythm of the rain.

It's pouring desire from skies
In magical shapes, red and bright.
A sunset is glowing my eyes
Nurturing with grace stars of night.

I wish I could fly over times
Of yearning for your arms, your smile
Through memories captured in rhymes
Of pushing your space in exile.

It's raining again over earth,
An angel is whispering psalms
To light my deep caves. A rebirth
Is gracing the peace in my palms.

Rain

My dear, this rain drops fears from skies
The bunch of clouds seems angry with the world
At the forefront of silence
Clumsily running between the sunsets
No longer the time is captured in mind.
Those normal things we got them once
Written deep down in heart
Are facing today's dilemmas
At the meeting with the burning wounds
Of mankind's ambition.

This rain, my dear, cries in my hands
Blinking the light reflection of eternity
Upon holiness in sight. So far is dark outside.
I shall pray gazing at the peaks
Of an evolved planet, crushed by the dust
For the angels to come and teach us
How peace is spelling in the heart
With golden letters penning through
One's faith, God's love, and hope's cart.

I Left the Path

I left the path…While dark got here
The angels were beneath the skies.
I felt their wings between your lies
Trying to save my mind from fear.

I run away from our nest
To ease the pain behind the door
Of what the shadows broke before
With thousands stabs upon my chest.

Yet steps are heavy on my way
Carrying with me a part of you,
The dawns bring memories to ray
Nostalgic stanzas under blue.

The evenings strike on thoughts we had
While catching moons between the stars
But still I run alone and sad
To find my heart under the scars.

Pipe Dream

I hold in myself, certain miserable reminiscences
Thoughtfully bleeding at the edge of my heart
Severing the mighty beatings of hope
From the intuitive sagacity deluge.
I carry with me, several sad memories,
Beige, olive, roasted and wacky, knotted up
Under the enchanted yearning sunrise
Of a wistful daydream…Just another pipe dream…

Our love turned out to be barely a shining tiny glass
Magnificently gleaming beneath the blaze of passion,
Sparkling with joy around the puzzle's desire,
Wonderfully melting our souls within a minty, savoury
delight.
Yet too soft in the blustery vernacular flow,
Of a manhood obliged custom, misunderstanding societal
touches.
Pressured by all and nothings,
Our years alas forced their way into thousands of pieces,
Collapsing relentlessly at our dusk, underneath the heavens.
Yet kneeing at the corners of hopelessness,
We were shaping back the glass,

'Till the sharp shards deeply wounded our shattered minds.
I carry with me a lacerated heart
Beneath a fresh, green, woody pipe dream
For the peace to hug me tight.

Worry

No dawns are yet coming to calm my old songs;
They beat on the fire same drums with their wrongs
Just spotting the panic, absurd and insane
While paying dilemmas with hassle to feign
New fret which is coming again and again.

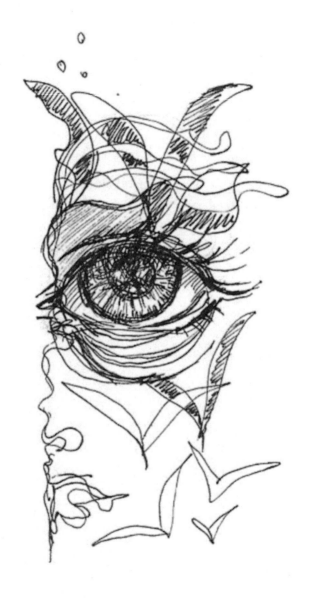

I Leave for You

I leave for you my secret message,
Written on playful wings of breeze,
It's yellow, sweet, with velvet touching,
Stirring with thirst the leaves of trees.
It may sing tunes below your windows,
Playing guitars in cherub's choirs,
Or might be waltzing between shadows,
Of undefined seraphic fires.

I leave for you my longing flashes,
With tears becoming sacred bliss,
Somewhere beneath of fondness' ashes,
Twisting my fate under stars' kiss.
And even if the storms would swamp them,
They may arrive to you in time,
Lighting those sparks somehow, I sensed,
Were stuck within the past's strong rhyme.

I leave for you my love as healing,
The wounds still bleeding in sunsets,
Carrying divine light's beams, revealing,
The crooked faces of regrets.
I leave, meanwhile, the trail to you,

To find yourself for a fresh start.
Holding my twinge beneath the blue,
I colour dreams somewhere apart.

Alabaster Jar

Tearing pieces of heart
Flowing away in ether
Melting auras between our souls
At the bridge of dimensions.
Love is washing the nights' dust
With the perfume of our memories.
Stars are pouring their teardrops
In the alabaster jar of my heart.

Ego Phobia

I am painting, evasively, lines on the paper…
My thoughts mirror the overseas
Marvels gather in me
Looking at how time is tying up
The magic into my forehead.

But my ego doesn't want to perceive me.
Close to the borders of fire
A demon inside is chanting
A nazar, shaking my chin.
I astray through the lines on the paper…

Bared stories invite me
To search more about myself
On the thoughts' darkness I twist
Wickets from ego phobia.
I drive through lines on the paper…

Apart

We used to smile at dawns,
At evenings we brought moon,
To join us in a waltz,
Of joy playing its tune.
We used to call it love,
With firestorms in heart,
But zest dismayed the dove,
Soaring ardours above,
Till found the peace apart.

Grace Is Walking on the Earth

Grace is walking on the earth,
Touching spirits, sparkling joy,
Charming woodland might enjoy,
Flowers' smiles on spring's rebirth.

Chirping songs are playing tunes,
Blessed with warmth and peaceful zest,
Trees are dressing to their best,
Happiness for honeymoons.

I might stay forever here,
Listening to the wildlife,
How the stories sense through life,
Upon hallowed tiers.

Mind's Corner

I stopped today at the thoughts' run,
A squint to give, then followed plan,
Routinely, with not much sun,
To light my lining's soul, just spots,
Through shadows, phobias, and dots.
Finding myself in question slots.

From where I'm coming every dawn,
Still where to run on daily base,
When colours beam from skies with grace,
And birds are dancing their run-on.
From yesterdays the past foregone,
Daring the mind to border on.

I paused today at gates of mind…
The brace of views embraces my doubt.
From darkness, nothing just brings-out,
Whatever things could mean in kind.
The question marks are to unblind,
What prejudices left behind.

Yearning's Refrain

Today I may paint all my dreams,
With colours to shine over dark,
With thoughts to embrace every spark,
Of meanings that flow through the streams.
Today I may bring to the light,
My joy and its story rewrite.

In mind I may sow seeds of trust,
And stick them to green of the life,
While stars caress the earth and adjust,
The hugs of the purple loosestrife.
In heart, spring is twirling the light,
Rebirthing the hope in my sight.

Today I may smile once again,
While love sings the yearning's refrain.

There Is September

There is September in my heart,
With peace fitting its golden suits,
Drawing some sweet on ripened fruits,
Lighting the best of every sight.

Angels are singing down from the skies
For hope to bring my soul on dance,
I smile amazed to every glance,
Of this September in my eyes.

Painting the calmness on the earth,
This afternoon is beaming blue,
On all my dreams becoming true.
There is September in my heart.

If Only

If only it'd be a mountain of love,
To rest on its crests, beneath the blue skies,
To wake up to life, to see the free dove,
Winged with such grace, defying the highs.

If only it'd be a valley of lust,
To lay on its grass, comforting the mind,
No matter how hard the night's monster's crust,
Would try to disguise the snuggles behind.

If only it'd be a chance to write down,
The emotions I keep at the core of my dreams,
The joy, the surprise, nurturing around,
A mystical tale and happiness' beams.

If only it'd be sunsets to hold hands,
Beneath the heavens of calmness and peace,
I could be alive to draw thousands plans,
On love's deepest wish and richest promise.

Speaking Your Truth

Out there of the dreams, near at the edge,
Of daily routine, feeding the pledge,
Tearing behind the smiling curtain,
Sweating details to get them certain.

Fearing conflicts on culture's belief,
Hiding yourself from freedom relief.
Out there of the dreams, look at the light,
How goes through the shade, spotting on right.

Finding the ways while facts spark your flame,
Being yourself with courage, no shame,
For feeling the faith through your inner peace.
Speaking your truth, love gets to release.

The Queue

Today we will stay in the queue
While embassy's staff count on rules
While nothingness just plays to the roof
Bringing the hope to the blue.

Today we will make up the queue.
Just six are allowed to breathe
Each day, no more space, to even seethe
Just follow the nights 'till get through.

Today we will spark in the queue.
The timing is beating with luck
While running the race over dark
Will embassy's door welcome through.

Today we may count in the queue
The hours we struggled for rights
While nobody cared for the lights
Which faded and got people screw.

Today we will seat over queue
While questions become rude to us
And love is accused being cursed
Because dared and no borders drew.

Mornings

He rings up mornings
Thriving the sunshine in room
And smiles he brings me
With his kind-hearted voice's comfort
Warming the distance between our yearning's corridors.
"Morning, bella ragazza
Ça va? Everything alright, fată frumoasă?" he asks me
Melting languages in a pot of lovingness
Adding cream of candied sounds
And a bit of magic hugged in the sweetened voice's inflection.
"Bien, merci, mon cheri."
My answer blooming through my heart's beams
Beating crazy in a teenager's style
Butterflying the aura of my wounded year.
"Tutto a posto?" I ask him, knowing that
Another day might get him another heavy bite.

We both are sharing hefty, bruised shadows from yesterdays.
Each of us from unalike paths but so matching
To the core's sorrow.
"Rendez-vous sur le chemin de la Tamise, today…"
"Sure, let's do it!"
The energy of water is amazingly reviving our depths

While our smiles are wholeheartedly speaking the same language
One of cheerful hope, of caring humanity
Despite the blue struggles from the past.
Yet victoriously chanting "We did it, honey, we did it!"
Somehow, in a good way, we survived
To the tormented current bloodshed
Slaughtering our mother lands
Running our days from the inconvenience of slavering
In others' fields of war
where we were marching the values
In the muddy camps of injustice.

Today we are carrying with us some weighty marks
Beneath, we still individually hold back our doubts.
A part of each other was nearly murdered by war
Yet still is watering the wild and delicate flowers of courage.
The telluric calling sparking the chambers of hearts
Is speaking of love for our hometowns…
Colours, flavours, our mother tongues
Nuances, shadows, sunrises, sunsets are painting
Memories capsuled in a fragile frame of lovingness
Helping us to shape our present language.

We are here, sipping our morning coffee in Paul's walk
Regarding the future with a sincere togetherness
Remembering always and forever
That the great, perfect unconditional love
Is only from the Creator
Sharing an entire universe

In the blossom of kindness, brotherhood
For humankind to keep the candles of compassion
Forever lifting the heart and soul.

A Nostalgia Song

This evening is seizing its pot with the stars
At the borders of wonder and magical skies
Thoughtfully gazing its colourful eyes
At the buildings outline, streets, trees, and cars.
Drawing amaze at my windows views
My neighbour is chanting melancholy blues.
His voice grasps with tender the walls in my room
Emphasizing emotions by Autumn's perfume.

A lyric is telling about being loved
Somewhere in the past, unclear season lost.
A longing is shaping the vibe in the song
Depicting her eyes as they came along
A story was crafted beneath charming moon
In joy, dreams, and vows pounding love's tune.
Craving emotions at gates of their lands
A fear yet flickered untrustworthy sands.

The wind starts to whisper its tracks at my door
Nurturing my silence in the deepest core.
Pairing the tune, the neighbour's voice grew
As story is holding no social clue
No fitting escape, no blue in the skies

No trust overcoming the fears in her eyes.
Some sort of the peril threatened their path.
I pause my gasp for a second, feeling the wrath.

The song slowly turns its way to a weep…
They found her, one morning, in the deepest sleep.
He knew in his heart how murdering game
Lays claim to restore the fake honour's name.
The next in their plan was his wicked head
Too daring to them, they wanted him dead.
It's heavy the air, I'm breathless, with tears
The walls sense the vibes, the wail, and the fears.

The evening is seizing the city's bright lights
From shadows are rising the marvels of nights.
I stare at the window, embracing the pray.
I no longer worry my falling away.
Emphatic and tender, the thoughts break the walls
The song turns its pitches on life's grateful calls.
His heart says the story releasing the pain
Of missing his love, his land, and his lane.

Hug Me

Hug me while cold nights surround
And doubts are the dinner for us
Apart from the stories' rebound
Of what we were striving to pass.

Hug me while hours stream hard
Still answering questions in mind
With waves of the light that regard
All our emotions behind.

Hug me while marvellous tales
From winters with splendid array
Will write our stories' details
Sparking the love on its way.

Hug me while nights turn on gleam
With moon smiling over the sky
With dawns which are catching the dream
Of having each other through fly.

Let's Play a Hugging Game

Let's play a hugging game,
Birds seemed to say,
We might share some food,
Some feelings for good,
Till earth will have healed,
Its most hurting wounds.

We might take on peace
For heart's pain to ease.
We might keep the hope,
In minds so could cope,
While panic absurd,
It's graving a wound,
To our mum-earth.
We her children birth,
Let's play hugging game,
For love to rename,
These moments of night,
In most springy light.

Let's play smiling cards,
In welfare regards.

Dreaming

A brilliant sight I'm dreaming and might
The colours of day will take it to light.
With spirits to play in mirrors away
The magical eyes do marvel the way.

One spot to create I'm dreaming and wait
To catch silver moons while glowing so great.
To draw all the dawns with joy and with peace
And craft shields of nights to a masterpiece.

I'm aiming to bright my darkness to light
To tear fears apart 'till get mornings right.

Remember Me

"Remember me when birds can't fly
And sorrow may seize your heart
The shadowy wings facing the sky
Through nights falling passion apart.

Remember me when things get wrong
And deeper the sadness may thrust
When whispers are singing their song
Spaced out on the cheerlessness dust.

Remember me closing your eyes
And see with your heart over edge.
I'm here, setting fires on skies
To spark through the wishes and pledge.

Remember me telling the dream!"
The hope murmurs calmly through days
Embracing my thoughts with its mean
When brightening life in its ways.

My Eyes Are Mirroring

My eyes are mirroring the sight
From years trapped within despair
With shadows striving to alight
The in-between to a new glare.
They saw the trail taking its course,
Reversing pain along the path,
Intensely looking for the force
Of love empowering the heart.

My eyes are mirroring the faith
Along those crooked, blurry days
Struggling to lower the ache's wraith
When nights were shattering the ways.
They saw the magic carving dreams
Beneath the wonder, near the blue
Reversing misery to beams
Of light joyfully coming through.

My eyes are mirroring the bliss
Of healing troublesome from past
Illuminating lands of peace
In my new heaven, blessed and vast.

Start Over Again

Grieve drags the tears.
Let them to flow
Washing the fears.
Breath deep inside
Finding yourself
Silence may shelf
Pieces of heart
Fractured apart.
Breaking hope's strain
Start over again!